DISNEY · PIXAR
FINDING NEMO

THE ESSENTIAL GUIDE

Large eyes, ever-watchful for danger

Tail fin (personal rudder)

Lucky fin

NEMO

MARLIN

CRUSH

PEARL

BLOAT

GILL

JELLYFISH

KATHY

CHUM

GURGLE

Disney · PIXAR
FINDING NEMO

THE ESSENTIAL GUIDE

DORY

MARLIN

Written by Glenn Dakin

CONTENTS

DIVE IN!

Welcome to Nemo's world, the big beautiful ocean.
It's an amazing place, full of some of the most brightly
colored sea creatures you'll ever meet. Join Marlin on his
journey from the Great Barrier Reef to Sydney, where he
meets the truly amazing animals that live in the warm
tropical waters of the Pacific Ocean. It is a sea teeming
with forgetful fish, friendly fish, happy fish, angry fish,
and extremely large fish! Dive into the adventure and if
you ever get stuck…just keep swimming!

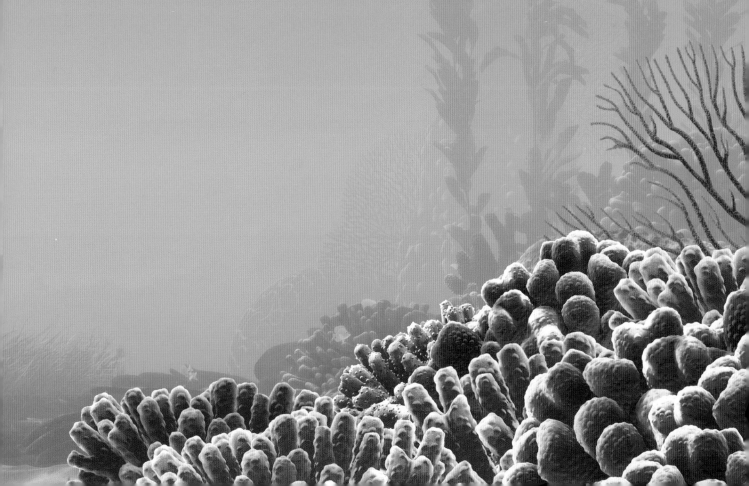

Nemo

Nemo is a little clownfish with big dreams. Despite being born with a withered fin, Nemo is destined to explore. As a toddler, he would beg for his dad to part the tentacles of their sea anemone home and glimpse the surrounding reef. Now, Nemo can't wait to start school—and he hopes one day to meet a shark!

Nemo's dorsal fin (the one on his back) keeps him floating upright and steady.

Home Life

Nemo's father, Marlin, keeps a watchful eye on his son. Growing up, they would stay safe inside their anemone home. Now that Nemo is six, it is time for him to start school. His dad says the ocean is not safe, but Nemo thinks he is ready to face the dangers.

CLOWNFISH
Home: Indian & Pacific Oceans
Adult Size: 3 in (7.5 cm)
Food: Not fussy eaters
Fact: Clownfish come in a wide range of bright colors.

Lucky fin

Nemo's right fin is much smaller than his left fin, so he swims a bit off-balance, but it doesn't slow him down. Marlin calls Nemo's right fin his lucky one. You see, Nemo's mother and siblings were taken away by a hungry barracuda when Nemo was an egg. Nemo survived, but was born with a damaged fin.

Fan coral

CLOWNFISH HOME

• A sea anemone makes a nice, safe home for you if you are a clownfish, but don't invite your pals around—your house might sting them!

• Clownfish are protected from the anemone's stings because they brush up against the tentacles every day to get used to them. Nemo has to brush every morning and night just like you!

• Clownfish are the only underwater animals who enjoy this special relationship with anemones.

Nemo's body shape is broken up by white stripes, making him harder for hungry predators to spot.

Nemo uses his tail to push himself along—like having a personal propeller.

Newcomer

Nemo's first day of school is more of an adventure than he ever could have imagined. He finds himself in a dentist's office fish tank complete with Hawaiian tiki heads and a bubbling volcano!

Fish Tank

Nemo meets a unique group of new friends in the dentist's fish tank. The tank's leader, Gill, takes Nemo under his fin and nicknames him "Shark Bait." Gill is from the ocean, like Nemo, and is determined to help Nemo get back to his dad. In fact, with Nemo's help, they might all escape!

Marlin

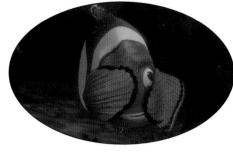

Nemo's dad Marlin is the most devoted parent on the reef. He's determined to look after Nemo and make sure that nothing bad happens to him. When a human diver catches Nemo, Marlin sets out on an heroic trek to find him, and becomes famous as the ocean's most daring dad. Marlin is proud of being a clownfish, and would be a funny one, too—if anyone ever let him finish a joke!

Devastated by a barracuda attack on his wife and family, Marlin constantly reminds his only son, Nemo, that "Danger is everywhere..."

Life Story

Marlin was born into a large family in Australia's Great Barrier Reef. One of 103 brothers and sisters, he was constantly trying to get attention by telling jokes—but no one seemed to be laughing. When he finally met a girl fish who found him funny, he decided to stop clowning around and married her pronto.

Marlin asks Nemo how many stripes he has whenever he thinks Nemo might be hurt. However, Nemo knows by now his dad always has three stripes!

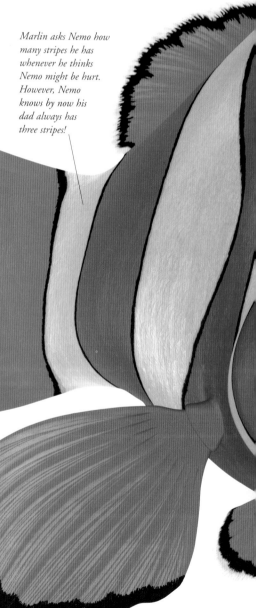

Marlin makes sure Nemo follows proper procedure when leaving their home. That is: Go out of the anemone, look for danger, swim back in, go out, look for danger, and back in again.... Often, Marlin forgets why they wanted to go out in the first place!

Trust Dory

Marlin meets a blue tang named Dory on his quest to find Nemo. They become friends. In fact, it is Dory who helps Marlin become a better father. She makes him realize that if he never lets anything happen to Nemo…nothing will *ever* happen to him!

A special layer of goo protects clownfish from anemone stings.

Marlin's large eyes are ever-watchful for danger.

MARLIN'S TOP FEARS

• Attack by barracuda: These spear-toothed eating machines shred first and ask questions later.

• No one will help him: All Marlin wants to do is find his son, but friendly fish can be hard to come by. He is especially frustrated by moonfish, who would rather do impressions than give directions.

• Becoming fish and chips: Marlin thinks that everything in the sea is waiting to eat him. However, after battling the ocean to rescue his son, he gets nicknamed Superfish…not bad for a fish from the reef.

Marlin is often amazed by his new friend Dory. They found a diver's mask that could be a clue to tracking down his son, they escaped a hungry shark, they survived an explosion…and she still has time to dream of bad haircuts!

Dory

She may seem to be the ocean's biggest bubblehead, but Dory is one feisty fish with hidden talents! Not much is known about her past, because she can't remember any of it! If you ask Dory about her family she'll probably say, "Sure, I have a big family…hey! Where'd they go?" But Dory always remembers to care about important things, like her friends and helping people in trouble.

REGAL TANG
Home: Indian and Pacific Oceans
Size: 10 in (25 cm)
Temperament: Energetic
Fish fact: Regal tangs enjoy playing with shells!

Regal tangs start out life yellow, just like Dory's tail is now; they gradually turn blue as they grow up.

Meeting Marlin

Dory and Marlin do not exactly start off as best friends. She promises she can lead him in the right direction to find Nemo. But when Marlin follows her, she forgets what she is doing and tells him to leave her alone!

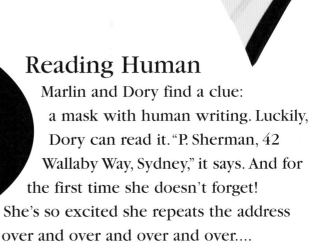

Reading Human

Marlin and Dory find a clue: a mask with human writing. Luckily, Dory can read it. "P. Sherman, 42 Wallaby Way, Sydney," it says. And for the first time she doesn't forget! She's so excited she repeats the address over and over and over and over….

Dory has bigger eyes than Marlin, as tangs get around more than clownfish and need to see in deeper, murkier places.

New Friends

Dory loves to play games. When a school of moonfish offers to play a game of charades, she can't resist. She is not very talented at charades, often mistaking a clam for an octopus. But it's a good thing she makes friends easily. These moonfish know the way to Sydney, Australia!

One of Dory's very special talents is the ability to speak whale. So far, she's mastered humpback, grey whale, and speaks three dialects of orca.

Dory points the tip of her fin toward her mouth when deep in thought.

DORY DATA

• Favorite song: Keep Swimming (written and composed by Dory!)

• Hobbies: Languages—along with whale, Dory can speak 42 fish dialects and is currently studying conversational plankton.

• Favorite food: Can't remember.

Tangs use their fins to zoom around real fast.

Coral Reef

The reef is a teeming metropolis, a great city of coral under the sea. It's the place where all the most weird and wonderful fish in the world get together to hang out… and, well, just be fish! It's also home to Nemo and his dad.

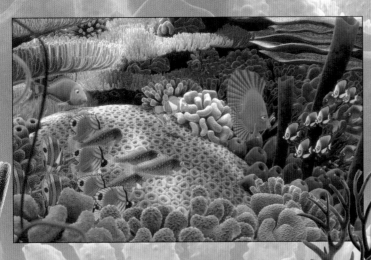

Reef Life

Life may look chaotic on the reef near Nemo's home, but really it's a well-organized society. There are swimming lanes instead of traffic lanes, coral stacks instead of apartment blocks, and nice sandy beds to sleep in at night.

The Great Barrier Reef is the world's largest coral reef. It is home to 1,500 species of fish and 400 different types of coral. The reef is young compared to other coral reefs—it is only 500,000 years old!

Hard corals provide homes for many busy little fish, who defend their own corners against strangers.

Nemo and Marlin live in a cozy anemone far from the open ocean.

REEF INFO

• Bright colors on a fish help it to attract a mate. Of course, there's no telling if they'll get along.

• Coral is the snack bar of the sea. Tiny sea plants grow with it and produce a constant source of food. Open 24-7, customers are never turned away, which proves there actually *is* such a thing as a free lunch!

• Anemones may look rooted to the spot, but if they run short of food, they can slurp off to a new picnic-spot by creeping along on their sucker-like bases—and then eat anything they find there!

• Spanish dancers are reef creatures that flamenco-dance their way out of trouble, flapping the hems of their brightly patterned "skirts" at unwanted followers.

Bright colors are helpful when crossing a busy fish stream at night.

Bert

Attention-grabbing shiny scales

Hutch

Maria the Spanish dancer

Tentacles used to smell food!

Organ pipe coral extend their feeders at night to grab passing snacks, and close during the day.

Brain coral look like human brains, but they're no smarter than any other coral.

Fish School

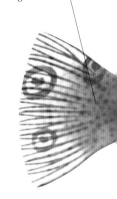

Sand color good for…well, mainly hiding in the sand

Fish love to get together in a school! Learning is fun with Mr. Ray in charge, who studied at the world-famous Barrier Reef Fish School. He loves to teach and also to sing. In fact, he sings while he teaches. "My songs have information, my songs have entertainment! Put them together and you get entertain-o-mation!" Judging by the class test score, Mr. Ray's teaching philosophy is paying off!

Pay Attention, Class!

Nemo's class is made up of all kinds of reef fish. The children all seem to get along, but Mr. Ray has two strict rules that every student must follow…learn and have fun!

RAYS
Home: Seabeds worldwide
Size: up to 28.8 ft (8.8 m) long
Animal group: Rays are related to sharks.
Fact: Rays are known to be intelligent creatures.

Eyes raised above head to see when napping on sandy bottoms

Wing-like fins for gliding slowly through the water

Welcome aboard! Mr. Ray can't imagine kids finding school boring. He thinks of them not as pupils, but as fellow explorers of the sea. As he likes to sing: "A life of science is filled with wonder, when facts of the sea are ours to plunder!"

Mr. Johannsen

Mr. Johannsen is the neighborhood grump. This cranky flounder hates when the reef kids play in his sandy yard. Fortunately, he is never able to catch the kids because he only has eyes on one side of his face!

Large, grumpy mouth

The other dads are surprised to see Marlin finally bringing Nemo to class. Sheldon's dad urges the kids to treat Nemo kindly. "Be nice! It's his first time at school!"

Jumping on Mr. Ray

Mr. Ray is so keen to show his pupils the world about them that he even doubles as a school bus. His wings provide the seating room—just don't stick kelp gum under the seats! Mr. Ray also takes the swim team to their tournaments. Go Fighting Plankton!

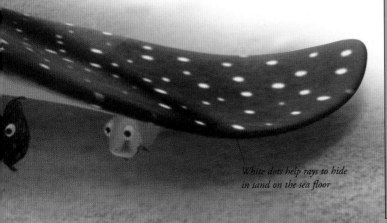

White dots help rays to hide in sand on the sea floor

SCHOOL LIFE

• The students at reef school don't have books. Instead of a blackboard, they draw pictures in the sand. At playtime, they use the sponge beds as a trampoline.

• Señor Seaweed is the school's music teacher. The school has lots of instruments, including sand-dollar tambourines, a kelp guitar, and a clam drum set. Unfortunately, clams don't appreciate being played!

• Kathy is the class techno-wiz. She dreams of one day inventing a synthetic oxygen lung so she can breathe above water and discover the uncharted territory above the sea.

Kathy

Strong teeth

School Friends

At first, Nemo's fellow pupils don't seem a very friendly bunch. Tad even tells Nemo he looks funny! But when Marlin explains to the other kids about his son's "lucky" fin, Nemo soon finds out that Pearl has one tentacle slightly shorter than the rest, and that poor Sheldon is "H2O intolerant" (water makes him sneeze!). So Nemo feels right at home with his new pals.

Is Nemo ready for school, or should he wait another five or six years, as his dad suggests?

False "eyespot" fools predators into thinking the fish is looking the other way

Some butterfly fish use their fins to leap right out of the water to catch flies!

BUTTERFLY FISH
Home: Coral reefs
Size: 5 in (12.5 cm) long
Food: Use long snout to poke in between rocks for food
Fact: Get their name from their habit of flitting around the reef

Tad

Tad is a long-nosed butterfly fish who loves to have fun. Because he is so smart, Tad gets bored easily and makes trouble just to get attention. Unfortunately, he often gets caught and has to clean the eraser sponges after class.

Making Friends

"C'mon Nemo!" Nemo soon finds out that his new friends are the coolest kids in the school. And maybe at last he'll discover whether everything his neighborhood friend, Sandy Plankton, says is true. Sandy told Nemo that turtles live to be a hundred!

Male seahorses give birth to babies!

On the very edge of the reef, Nemo and his new friends excitedly discuss the sight of a mysterious floating object from the world of humans. Sandy Plankton says it's called a butt. It's actually a boat. Wouldn't it be cool to try and touch it? Big mistake, kids!

Sheldon

A kid seahorse, Sheldon likes to gallop around the reef with his pals. His sneezing sends him backwards all the time, which means he is always the last one to touch base in a game of tag.

Curly tail used to grip onto seaweed

Octopuses propel themselves along by sucking water into their bodies and blowing it out again.

SEAHORSE
Home: Warm waters
Size: 2–14 in (5–36 cm)
Fact: Seahorses swim upright, rapidly waving their fins to move themselves

THE OTHER DADS

• Tad's dad, Phil, is a long-nosed butterfly fish who had a hard time himself when his first kid started school. Ten kids later, he is an old pro.

• Pearl's pa, Ted, is a flapjack octopus. He thinks it is a pity that Marlin is a clownfish who isn't funny.

• Sheldon's dad, Bob, is a seahorse who always keeps a healthy supply of slimy kelp tissues on hand for his H$_2$O-intolerant son. By the way, he doesn't appreciate being called "Pony Boy."

Pearl

Pearl is a little flapjack octopus. Her friends like to scare her because octopuses spurt black ink when frightened. (Pearl hates inking in public.) Nonetheless, she is one of the most popular kids at school and is the star soccer player. She has eight great feet!

OCTOPUS
Home: Atlantic and Pacific Oceans
Size: up to 18 in (45.5 cm)

The Drop-off

Welcome to the edge. This is where the reef ends and the unknown realms of the ocean begin. Marlin thought it would be a great place to raise his kids, until they were taken away by a barracuda. When he finds out that his son is headed there on his first school trip, Marlin immediately chases after him.

Nemo!

The Drop-off is the perfect place for divers to anchor their "butts" and explore the reef. Nemo dares to "touch the butt" to spite his father and impress his new friends. But everything goes wrong when a diver captures him by surprise.

Plate coral provides handy shade on a sunny day, but watch out—dark corners are a great place to meet up with some nasty predators....

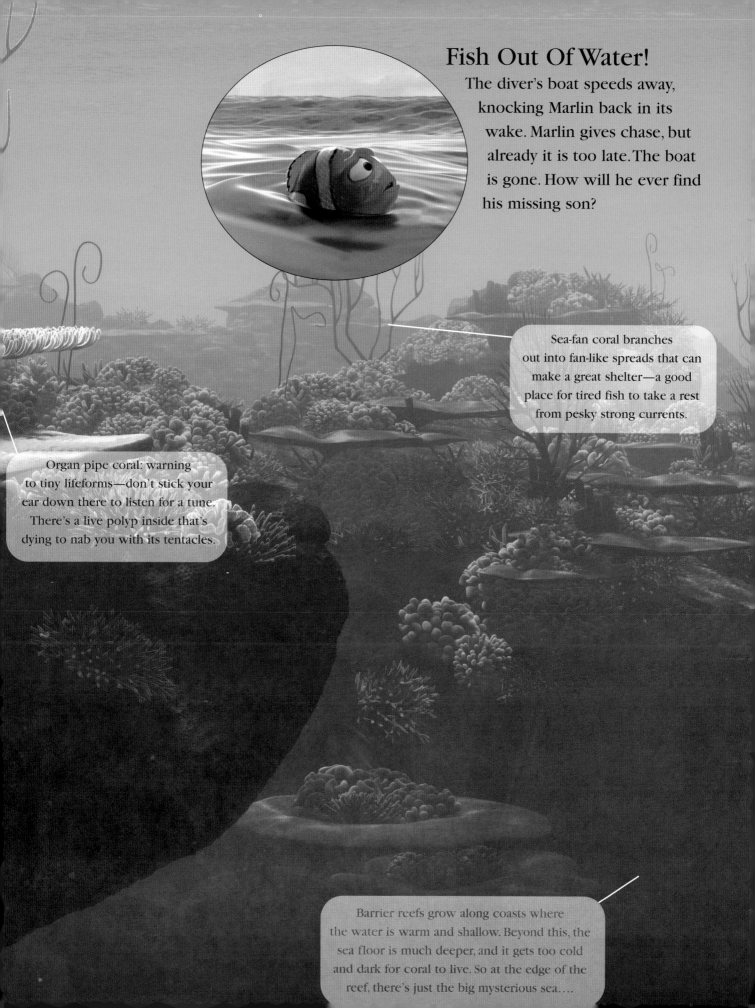

Fish Out Of Water!

The diver's boat speeds away, knocking Marlin back in its wake. Marlin gives chase, but already it is too late. The boat is gone. How will he ever find his missing son?

Sea-fan coral branches out into fan-like spreads that can make a great shelter—a good place for tired fish to take a rest from pesky strong currents.

Organ pipe coral: warning to tiny lifeforms—don't stick your ear down there to listen for a tune. There's a live polyp inside that's dying to nab you with its tentacles.

Barrier reefs grow along coasts where the water is warm and shallow. Beyond this, the sea floor is much deeper, and it gets too cold and dark for coral to live. So at the edge of the reef, there's just the big mysterious sea....

Fin shortens as fish ages—so the youngest are often the tallest!

The Tank Gang

When Nemo wakes up in a dentist's fish tank, he doesn't know what to expect. Certainly not the group of stir-crazy fish who greet him—the Tank Gang. And every gang needs a mastermind to cook up ingenious plans. Let's meet Gill, and some of the wacky characters who live at 42 Wallaby Way, Sydney.

Thin body for slipping in amongst the cracks and crevices of coral reefs

Withered fin from the poor conditions in a previous fish tank

Scars from landing on surgical instruments after failed escape attempt

Gill

"Fish aren't meant to be in a box, kid…it does things to you!" That sums up the attitude of this moorish idol fish who always has an escape plan up his sleeve. Gill knows no fear. He is confident that, as he says, "all drains lead to the ocean."

Finest molded plastic

MOORISH IDOL

Home: Tropical waters
Temperament: Moody fish that fights back if cornered
Size: 8 in (20 cm)
Fun fact: Colorful stripes help moorish idols hide in the reef.

Gold-effect tooth

The tank's plastic skull serves as a cozy sanctuary for Gill. It reminds him of home. However, this version is made in Japan from recycled materials.

HUMBUG

Home: Tropical waters

Temperament: Peaceful

Size: 3 in (8 cm)

Deb's reflection (but don't tell her!)

Jacques spends many hours hanging out in the tank's diving helmet. It makes him feel like a deep-sea explorer.

Jacques

Jacques is a cleaner shrimp. He was once the official cleaner of the President of France's fish tank. When Jacques retired, he was given as a gift to the Prime Minister of Australia, who in turn gave Jacques to his dentist.

CLEANER SHRIMP

Size: 2 in (5 cm)

Fact: Cleaner shrimp "clean" fish by eating tiny animals off them!

Deb

Deb is a black and white humbug who loves her own reflection—not that she's vain, she just thinks it's her identical sister, Flo. A reflection follows you around loyally, and when you're feeling low, it does too!

GILL'S PAST

• Gill was a carefree reef-rat as a kid. He fell in with a gang of adventurous fish who set out to see if they could swim around the world before dinner. Guess what—they got hungry and came right back home.

• It was on one of these outings that Gill and his mates were captured and ended up in a pet store. One by one, his friends accepted their fate. But Gill refused to be tamed, and believes that, like Nemo, he can get back his freedom by returning to the ocean, his home, and his family.

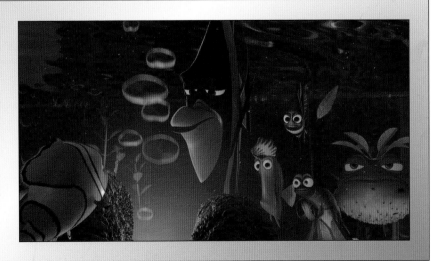

More Gang!

Ever thought how dull it would be to be stuck in a fish tank all day? Well, think again—being part of this kooky crowd makes captivity almost seem fun…but the one thing that keeps them all going is the eternal hope of escape. Well, that and placing bets on how many fillings each customer is going to need!

Spines point outward at right angles to his body, so Bloat doesn't pop himself!

Bloat

Bloat is a short-tempered blowfish. He looks just like a regular fish until he gets riled, and then he literally blows up with rage! When Bloat was little, his big brother used to bat him around like a volleyball—and that just made him angrier. Blowfish are one of nature's most amazing creations, but Bloat doesn't have an inflated view of himself!

Fins used for flapping

Inflation is possible because of elastic skin and no ribs

Bloat looks a lot less alarming when he is deflated. Blowfish use their blowing-up gimmick to scare off undersea bullies.

Spines are poisonous

22

The tank's treasure chest unleashes bubbles at a rate of 100 per second.

Bubbles

Bubbles likes to chase bubbles. That's why he's named Bubbles. The source of Bubbles' bubbles is a treasure chest at the bottom of the fish tank. Bubbles rarely catches any bubbles.

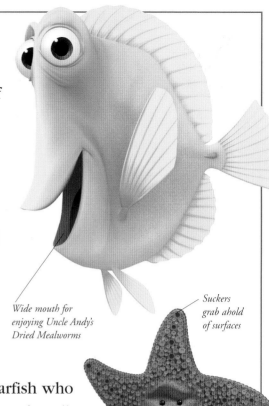

YELLOW TANG
Size: 8 in (20 cm)
Behaviour: Dart about at great speed!

Wide mouth for enjoying Uncle Andy's Dried Mealworms

Suckers grab ahold of surfaces

Neurotic fin-in-mouth gesture

Peach

Peach is a starfish who clings to the tank wall all day long. She enjoys counting how many coffees the dentist has had and predicting his next toilet break.

STARFISH
Home: Sea floors
Fact: If a starfish's arm is cut off, it will grow back again within a year!

Gurgle

Gurgle grew up in a crummy pet shop. His tank was choked with slime. In fact, he thought he was green until the day he was put in a plastic bag for delivery to another tank, and the gunk was washed off. Now he's sworn never to be dirty again!

Royal gramma fish are known for their rainbow colors.

ROYAL GRAMMA
Home: Coral reefs
Size: 3 in (7 cm) long
Temperament: Like their own space

After Nemo is initiated into the tank's club and given the nickname "Shark Bait", Gill explains that he is the key player in their escape plan. Is Nemo up for the task?

Tank Life

To outsiders, it's just a fish tank in dentist Philip P. Sherman's office. But to Gill and the gang, it's home. With its bubbling electric volcano, Polynesian village, and plastic gravel, it's a strange place to live—with some very bizarre rules and rituals....

Dental Diagnostics

To the gang, dentistry is a serious spectator sport. They have learned all the jargon and can spot a tricky molar extraction diagnosis from X-rays at over 10 yards. Peach is the real dentistry expert. She hopes that one day she'll be called on to spring into action and finish a root canal that the dentist can't handle.

The fish sometimes use pebbles to bet on a patient's diagnosis.

Tiki heads were found in a discount bin at Bob's Fish Mart

Aqua Scum 2003®
AS2K3®

hyper accelerated robotic pump

auto filtration compartment

purified fluid expulsion grill

world wide web communication housing

digital mainframe

solar power generator

nanotech filtration system

scan data storage motherboard

the "LASER" primary sensory device

fluid dynamic intake grill

THE AQUA SCUM 2003

• Gill's plan is to jam the gears of the tank's filter system with a pebble. With the filter broken, the water will get dirty. Then, when the tank is cleaned manually, the fish will be put into plastic bags and they can roll out the window to freedom.

• This ingenious plan fails when the Aqua Scum 2003 is installed. It's an all-purpose, self-cleaning, maintenance-free, salt-water purifier.

• This device laser-scans the tank every five minutes, so it will never become dirty again! Gill's master plan is ruined... but on the bright side, the water does feel kind of softer on the scales.

The tank sits in the wall between the lobby and the exam room. The fish hold secret meetings at the volcano they call Mt. Wannahockaloogie. It is here that Nemo swims through the ring of fire (actually a stream of bubbles) to join the gang! "Ah-hoo-wah-hee. Ah-ho-ho-ho!"

Mount Wannahockaloogie adorns the lobby side of the tank.

PH-balanced saltwater

Fake coral remind the fish of home

Chuckles used to spy on the dentist from the ship's crow's nest.

Tank Ship

The tank's pirate ship faces the exam room. The fish usually avoid the ship because it reminds them of their old pal, Chuckles, who was a present for the dentist's niece, Darla, last year. Unfortunately, Darla shook the bag too hard and Chuckles went belly up. The tank gang tried to lower the flag to half mast, but sadly it doesn't move.

Dentist's Lobby

With its sailing-theme wallpaper and hanging life preservers, Philip Sherman's lobby says a lot about the man. For Philip Sherman, dentistry is a way to support his true love: scuba-diving! He would prefer a deep-sea dive to a molar extraction any day. However, Phil continues the family line of Sherman dentists. His great-great-grandfather opened the practice on Wallaby Way in 1895.

Gums Most likely to Recede Award

Society of Denture Wearers of New South Whales — *Toothless Grin Award*

P. Sherman graduated second from last in his class, but the awards on his wall tell a different story.

Buzz Lightyear action figure   *Darla's drawings*   *M is for Monster book*   *Fish tank in specially built hatch*

Lobby Life

P. Sherman is known as a family dentist. When he took over the practice from his father, he redecorated the lobby to appeal to patients of all ages…and his sea-going interests. With a fish tank, toys, and plenty of reading material, there is something to please everyone.

THE DIVING DENTIST

- Dr. Sherman often goes diving with his old chums from dental school at Alice Springs University. They call him "Skip"—since he had a lucky skipper cap he would wear during exams.

- Philip Sherman is the captain of his dive boat, *The Aussie Flosser*. He hopes to sail around the world when he retires from dentistry.

- Pet peeve: having to buy sugar-free products all the time in case he bumps into another dentist in the supermarket.

Face mask—always label clearly with your name and address!

Luminous stripes make Dr. Sherman look slimmer

Philip Sherman never takes fish from the reef except when he finds one "struggling for life" with an injured fin.

Luxury brace set, received at special discount

Darla

Darla Sherman is a second grader from Waltzing Matilda Primary School in Sydney. She loves fish and always shakes the bag with excitement when she gets one. However, she thinks her uncle has very sleepy fish. Maybe the silly gas gets to them, too?

P. Sherman's appointments calendar

Chuckles

Lucky Darla always gets a free check-up from her uncle on her birthday...and a present. Last year, after Darla's fishy present died, her uncle bought her now-favorite sweatshirt which says "Rock 'n' Roll Girl."

Overalls stained with brown milk after accident with bowl of Chock-O's sugar-coated caramel cube cereal

Exam Room

Here it is—Philip Sherman's exam room, where all the action takes place. Many famous patients have come through the doors of this room for a painless root canal or cavity filling. It is a good thing that the fish in the tank can't talk!

With no wife or kids to lavish gifts upon, Dr. Sherman pours all his money into toys, whether it's an ocean-going dive boat, the latest Deluxe Relax-o-matic Dental Activity Facilitator (that's the chair), or just a brand-new pair of *really* sharp tools.

High-tech oral implement

TANK HOOD #A65412385-48981
© 2000 Patent Pending
Manufactured in Sydney, Australia

The fish tank—patients like to have something to fix their attention on when they are "in the chair"

Your Mission

Should you wish to accept, your instructions for escape are detailed below. Good luck, fish.

1. Once in your plastic bag, roll across the counter to the ledge and out the window. (Make sure the window is open before attempting.)

2. Aim for the awning to cushion the drop.

3. At the street, look both ways before bag-rolling.

4. Bounce over the pilings and into the harbor to the big blue!

Mission accomplished!

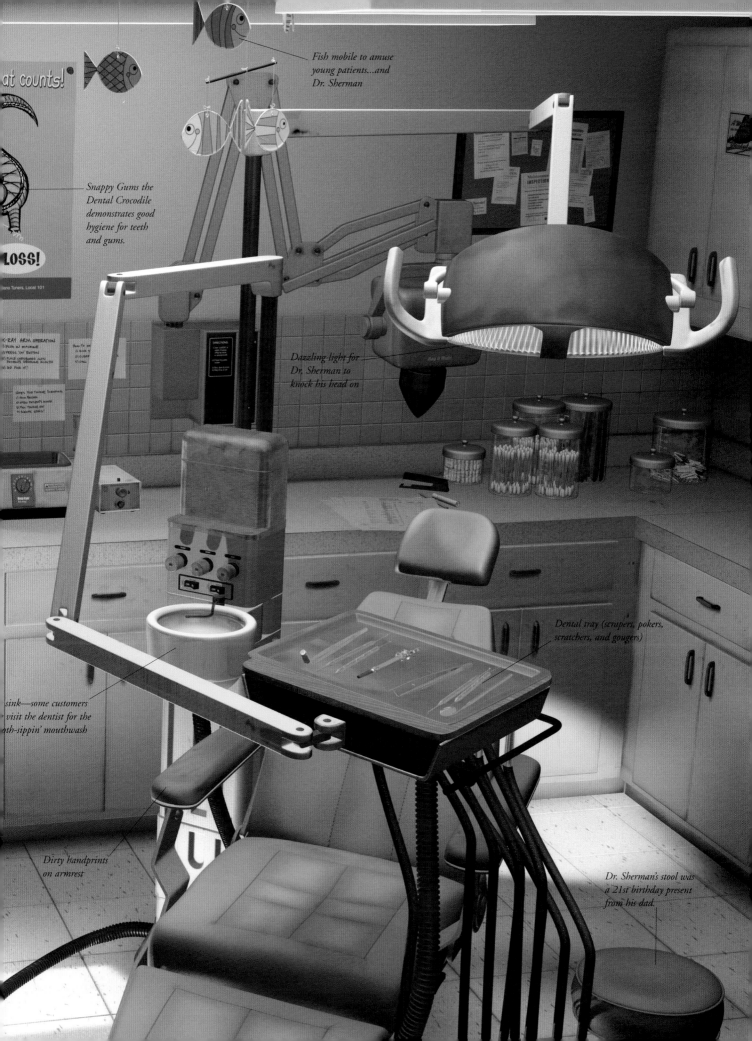

Fish mobile to amuse
young patients...and
Dr. Sherman

Snappy Gums the
Dental Crocodile
demonstrates good
hygiene for teeth
and gums.

Dazzling light for
Dr. Sherman to
knock his head on

Dental tray (scrapers, pokers,
scratchers, and gougers)

sink—some customers
visit the dentist for the
oth-sippin' mouthwash

Dirty handprints
on armrest

Dr. Sherman's stool was
a 21st birthday present
from his dad.

Bruce

G'day mate! The lovable guy with the chainsaw smile is Bruce, a great white shark born and raised on the Great Barrier Reef. He looks like a real terror of the deep, but appearances can be deceiving—Bruce is a shark with a crusade! He has created a vegetarian group, because he wants to change the bad image sharks have for chewing up just about everyone they meet. His slogan is "fish are friends…not food!"

Bruce is a persuasive public speaker at his anti-meat-eating meetings. Despite ravenously chasing Marlin and Dory, he will always consider them members of his group. If they get into any future scrapes, they'll have a cool buddy to call on!

Tail is used for steering, moving, and speed control

GREAT WHITE
Home: Warm waters
Size: About 13 ft (4 m) long
Favorite food: Bruce thrives on vegetarian kelp salad but most sharks eat fish.
Fact: Great whites have 3,000 teeth!

Body built like a torpedo for speed

Friends For Life
When Bruce meets Marlin and Dory, he is keen to make a good impression—not eating them is a good start. He invites them to his next party, which is held in a sunken submarine.

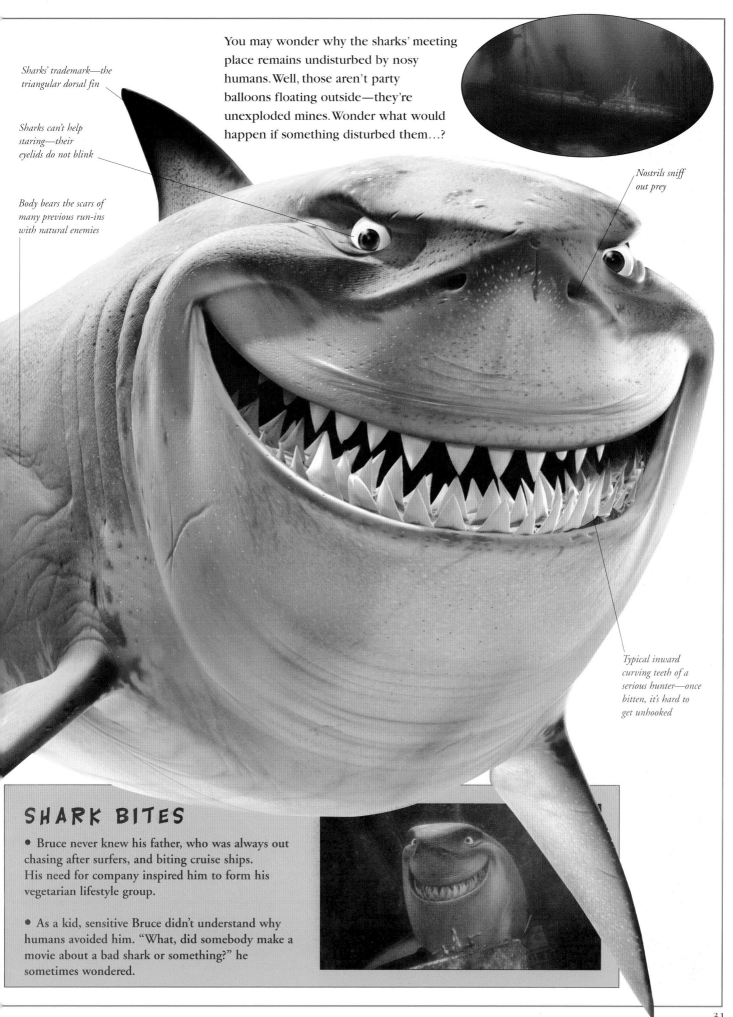

You may wonder why the sharks' meeting place remains undisturbed by nosy humans. Well, those aren't party balloons floating outside—they're unexploded mines. Wonder what would happen if something disturbed them…?

Sharks' trademark—the triangular dorsal fin

Sharks can't help staring—their eyelids do not blink

Body bears the scars of many previous run-ins with natural enemies

Nostrils sniff out prey

Typical inward curving teeth of a serious hunter—once bitten, it's hard to get unhooked

SHARK BITES

• Bruce never knew his father, who was always out chasing after surfers, and biting cruise ships. His need for company inspired him to form his vegetarian lifestyle group.

• As a kid, sensitive Bruce didn't understand why humans avoided him. "What, did somebody make a movie about a bad shark or something?" he sometimes wondered.

Anchor & Chum

Bruce, Anchor, and Chum met at a feeding frenzy. Being good guys deep down, they felt racked with guilt at pigging out on so many of their finny brethren, and decided to form a vegetarian shark society. They take it in turns to bring snacks to their weekly meetings. Sushi is frowned upon, but a nice seaweed sandwich keeps them satisfied.

Today's meeting is Step Five: Bring a Fish Friend. Chum, unfortunately, seems to have misplaced his friend.

Anchor

This happy hammerhead is self-conscious about the irregular shape of his head, and appreciates his mates not teasing him about it. He always avoids swimming with swordfish and spiral-toothed narwal, because he thinks that together they'll look like an underwater toolbox.

Super hearing—hammerheads can even hear air-bubbles moving through the water (so be careful what you eat before diving!)

Hammerheads use their tail fins to twist and turn.

HAMMERHEAD
Home: Warm waters
Size: 11.5 feet (3.5 m) long
Shark fact: Like to have "fun" with stingrays by pinning them down with their hammerheads and "playfully" nipping their wings!

Big belly

Each tooth is jagged, making it quite unreasonably sharp.

The highlight of any club meeting is the chance to offer up your testimonial and tell your fish brothers about your problems. Remember, you are a nice shark, not a mindless eating machine.

The sharks are keen to show their enthusiasm for the fish-free diet, none more so than Anchor. He loves giving things up, and even tried to give up swimming once! But since sharks need to swim to breathe, this idea didn't last long.

Experts are still not 100% sure, but they think the wide-apart eyes and nostrils help the shark detect prey with pinpoint accuracy.

BITE-SIZE FACTS

• Sharks suffer from a serial-killer image in the human world. In fact, they are much less vicious toward us than you might think. Some experts think sharks only attack people because they mistake them for seals or dolphins, which it is easy to do when you're hungry.

• The toughest part of being in the group is when one of your buddies loses control. Then it's your job to intervene and keep him on track with the program. You should also apologize profusely to the fish your friend is trying to eat.

• Blenny is a new guest at the sharks' fish-friendly meetings. Anchor befriended him against his will during a new recruitment drive.

Blenny is still overcoming his fear of sharks.

Blenny

MAKO SHARK
Home: Warm waters
Character: Unpredictable
Size: 8 ft (2.4 m) long
Top speed: 22 mph (35 kph)
Hobbies: Stalking dolphins (who think they're so cute)

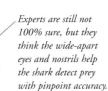

Chum

Secretly something of an upper-class shark, Chum is a mako who likes to hang with Bruce and Anchor. He puts on a rough-sounding accent he learned from a caretaker at his posh predator boarding school. Chum worries he'll be spotted one day by his hoity-toity friends, fraternizing with the local reef-raff.

Souvenir of a recent tussle with a fisherman (Chum won)

Dark eyes allow Chum to look smarter than he really is

Makos pride themselves on having the sleekest bodies of all sharks.

Dapper white underside sets off the dark gray-blue top well

Huge, curved teeth—Chum's pals often call him "old snaggletooth" (but not to his face, of course)

Sunken Sub

Lying on the ocean floor the submarine is a relic of an old sea battle. Its once shining corridors are now rusted, and have become a battleground in the fight against eating fish. The sharks meet here to battle their hunger for fish and change their bad image To do this, they must first change themselves.

They cram just about everything into a sub including the kitchen sink —and here it is.

The sharks hold meetings in the sub's dining room, known as the mess hall. Actually the whole sub is a bit of a mess, but that's another story We ve taken the liberty of adding another hole in the ship to show you Marlin and Dory's race through the sub from the hungry Bruce.

The mess hall—bring a friend!

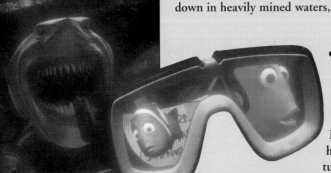

UNDERWATER HANG-OUT

• The submarine was lost during World War II. It went down in heavily mined waters, but suffered surprisingly

• The sharks have been using this wreck as a hang-out for years. But it is about to be relocated…by a massive explosion. When Dory and Marlin needed a safe place to hide from Bruce, maybe a torpedo tube wasnt the best idea ever….

Let Us Out of Here!

The frantic chase through the submarine leads to a sudden dead-end, which is not what Marlin and Dory were looking for—especially with a shark on their tail. Marlin desperately searches for an escape when Dory reads a word she pronounces as "Es-Cah-Pay." Funny, it's spelled just like "Escape."

Deck-mounted cannon, now home to a small family of reclusive peanut worms.

Number and name of vessel, long since covered by marine growth.

Torpedo tube—try to avoid being locked in one.

Barnacles: crustaceans which will grow on just about anything, even whales… and subs!

- - → Marlin's and Dory's route

- - → Bruce's route

The Abyss

Anglerfish use an
elongated spine as
a fishing rod.

Welcome to the place where it's
always night! At the bottom of the
ocean, there's no light—just a cold,
inky blackness filled with creatures
that are the stuff of nightmares.
The trouble is, these nightmares
are real! The abyss dwellers are
delighted to see anyone that
ventures down from the seas
above…because it's always nice
to have a midnight snack.

Millions of glowing
bacteria live inside the
"lure," creating a
lightbulb effect.

Small eyes, as there is usually
nothing to see in the abyss, and
never anything good on TV

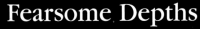

Fearsome Depths

When Marlin and Dory swim into the darkness
of the abyss searching for the diver's mask that
could lead them to Nemo, Dory becomes
disoriented. She thinks Marlin's voice is her
conscience. It's a creepy place that plays tricks
on your mind—like seeing ghostly lights….

Teeth curve inwards
to ease prey in, and
prevent a swift exit

A friendly light seems to call to you,
inviting you to come and bask in its
glow. Down in that murk, it's the most
welcome sight you've ever seen. You
want to get closer and reach out to it.
SNAP! You just got caught by the
fisherman of the abyss. He's the deep-sea
anglerfish, and you took the bait!

ANGLERFISH FACTS

• Anglerfish make their living not by means of speed or power, but by a clever gimmick. Rather than chasing after a fish, they dangle a lantern in front of their heads to lure it near to their mouth. Then they gobble up the mesmerized creature!

• In the anglerfish world, the female rules. She grows nearly 20 times bigger than the male and does all the hunting—only females have glowing lures. Puny males rely on her for everything— food, security, setting the VCR....

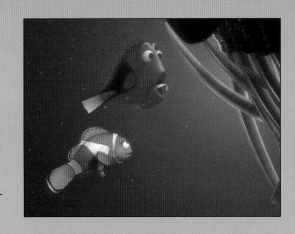

Dark body stays hidden in the darkness

Stomach can stretch to fit in extra-big dinners

ANGLERFISH
Home: At the darkest and scariest depths of the ocean
Size: (females) 4 ft (1.2 m)
(males) 2.5 in (6.3 cm)
Temperament: Anglerfish are eating machines—not fun-loving at all!

Trapped

Marlin didn't take "Escaping an Anglerfish 101" in school, but he still manages to trap the anglerfish with a diver's mask. He finally learns what the mask says, but the more immediate lesson is never taunt anglerfish!

Moonfish

No other crowd of fish enjoy hanging out together like moonfish. They are the impersonators of the sea, using their talents to amuse their friends and frighten their enemies. They once scared off a barracuda by creating the likeness of a hammerhead shark. This was great until they got invited to a feeding frenzy by a bunch of *real* hammerheads!

Marlin tells Dory he wants to finish the journey on his own, which upsets her. Fortunately, when the moonfish swim by to ask her what's wrong, Dory has already forgotten why she was crying.

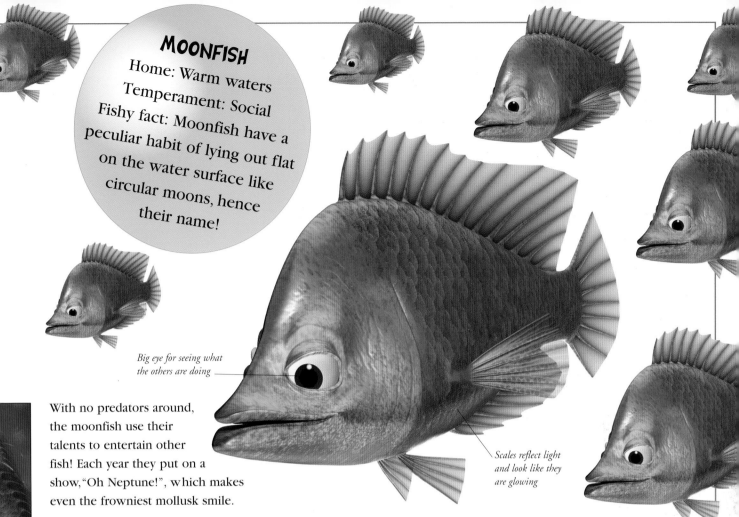

MOONFISH
Home: Warm waters
Temperament: Social
Fishy fact: Moonfish have a peculiar habit of lying out flat on the water surface like circular moons, hence their name!

Big eye for seeing what the others are doing

Scales reflect light and look like they are glowing

With no predators around, the moonfish use their talents to entertain other fish! Each year they put on a show, "Oh Neptune!", which makes even the frowniest mollusk smile.

Helping Out
At first, the moonfish play games with Marlin, making him realize what a grumpy-gills he can be sometimes. However, once the moonfish learn of Marlin and Dory's quest to find Nemo they're happy to help. They even use their talents to warn Dory to go through the big trench up ahead, not over it. Good call! Now if only she can remember their advice....

IMPRESSIONISTS

• These guys' slick routine is the result of endless practice. Giving directions is easy, but becoming an arrow to point the way is hard work.

• You want difficult? Then how about this...the moonfish do an impression of the Sydney Opera House.

• These jokers give Marlin a hard time at first because he's a clownfish. Moonfish work on their comedy hard, and are jealous of a clownfish's natural talent for being funny. Lucky Marlin didn't tell any jokes and spoil the illusion....

Jellyfish

They look like mindless blobs of jelly, meandering aimlessly through the ocean. But rumor has it that jellyfish are really the most intelligent creatures in the sea. It is claimed they spend all day stumping each other with complicated math problems and riddles!

Round umbrella-like body moves the animals with a pumping motion

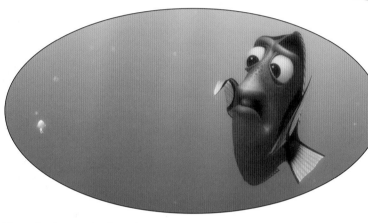

Bad Squishy!

When Dory comes across a baby jellyfish, she calls the little cutie "Squishy" and wants to claim it has her own—until it stings her! Immune to its stings, Marlin shoos the baby away, unaware that jelly moms and dads are about to surround them.

Long tentacles are covered in stingers to stun prey

Flaps called oral arms line the jellyfish's mouth and are used to eat prey

JELLYFISH TRENCH

• Nice Trench. When Dory and Marlin reach the jellyfish trench, Dory has a feeling that they should swim through it, but she cannot remember why. Unfortunately, Marlin distracts her and they swim over the trench into the jellyfish forest.

• Jellyfish are very proud of their tentacles. They grow them as long as they can, and hate having a bad tentacle day!

• Clownfish joke: How do you make a jellyfish laugh?
Answer: Give him ten tickles (tentacles)!

Making Friends

Dory thinks that jellyfish are fun. To her, they are big gelatinous swimming trampolines. She is just too forgetful for her own good, and Marlin has to think fast if they're going to escape from the jelly-jam.

Jellies have long stinging tentacles that can stun their prey. And if the two fish friends don't escape quickly, they've had their chips!

JELLYFISH

Home: Oceans worldwide
Size: up to 8 ft (2.4 m) across
Most dangerous: Australia's box jellyfish can kill a person!
Fact: Jellyfish are not fish, but are related to sea anemones.

How do you escape from a great slobbery mass of jellyfish? The trick is to bounce on their tops, because their blobby heads don't sting. See, it always pays to use your head—or someone else's!

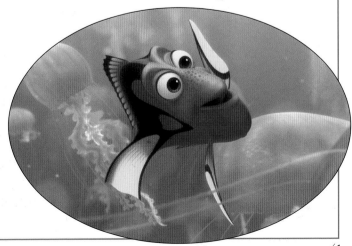

Turtles

Surfing the ocean currents, the turtles are the coolest dudes in the sea. They love to swim, bask in the sun, and ride the waves. But turtles are tough guys, too. Their shells can survive the battering of stormy seas, and they can live to incredible ages. Nemo has always wanted to know exactly how long they live. Marlin is lucky enough to meet one who is 150 years old, and still young.

Crush

A hippie turtle, Crush first decided to settle down and have kids at the super-young age (for a turtle) of 57. He is dedicated to the lifelong pursuit of riding the perfect current. He loves teaching his little dudes to surf the gnarly currents of life without wiping out.

Little dudes listen wide-eyed to Marlin's story

Back flippers are for steering

Shell is a streamlined shape to slice through the water, which means greater cruising speed

TURTLE EYES

• Turtles are attracted to bright lights. When they are born on a beach, the babies sometimes mistakenly head toward street or house lights, instead of the sea.

• Tears sometimes drop from turtles' eyes, but it doesn't mean they're unhappy. They just drink a lot of salty sea water and have to drain out the salt through their eyes.

Squirt

Crush's son, Squirt, learned to surf the waves at an early age. Like all turtles, he was born on a beach and had to make his way back to his parents in the sea, braving hungry crabs and snapping seagulls. Now he knows no fear!

Squirt's favorite food is yummy seaweed.

Worn out from escaping the jellyfish, Marlin and Dory might have ended up nowhere if Crush hadn't guided them into the E.A.C.—the East Australian Current. It's like an express highway through the ocean and ends up in the waters close to Sydney.

Strong beak for shredding seaweed to snack-size bites and snacking on the odd tough-skinned strawberry jellyfish

Strong front flippers beat the water almost like wings

Goodbye Dudes

Waterways can get a bit congested and the E.A.C. is no exception. Hundreds of turtles and sea creatures ride the E.A.C. for miles to reach their next destination. When exiting the current to Sydney, one must always follow proper exiting technique. Remember: rip it, roll it, and punch it.

The Whale

When Marlin and Dory are in need of directions to Sydney, Dory spots someone she can ask. Under the sea, distances can be deceptive...the "little fella" that she calls out to turns out to be the biggest living creature in the whole ocean—the blue whale!

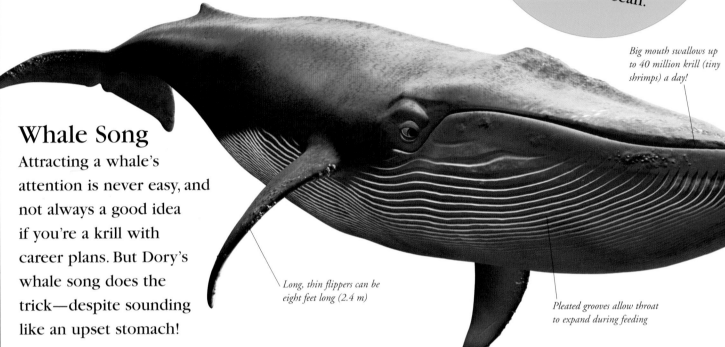

Big mouth swallows up to 40 million krill (tiny shrimps) a day!

Whale Song

Attracting a whale's attention is never easy, and not always a good idea if you're a krill with career plans. But Dory's whale song does the trick—despite sounding like an upset stomach!

Long, thin flippers can be eight feet long (2.4 m)

Pleated grooves allow throat to expand during feeding

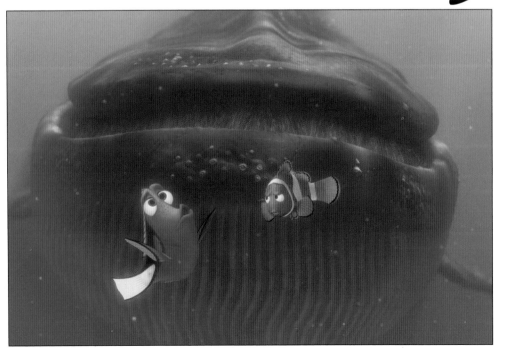

Inspection

Has the whale heard the story of Marlin and his quest to find Nemo? Maybe so, as whales have a way of picking up gossip from hundreds of miles away, in their extraordinary songs. While our heroes are debating their next move, the kindly leviathan cruises up and checks out his future passengers.

In the Whale

After Marlin is swallowed up by the whale, he thinks he will never get to tell Nemo how old sea turtles are, but Dory remains optimistic. She convinces Marlin that everything is going to be alright…and it is! The whale shoots them out of his blowhole and into Sydney harbor.

Whales are big enough to swallow tugboats. But they feed on one of the tiniest creatures of the sea: krill. They strain them out of the water through their baleen, the special plates inside their mouths.

Shell helps crabs survive stormy waters and protects their insides

Bernie

Skeleton is on the outside of body

Powerful claws for holding food…and tearing wrappers off candy bars!

UNDER SYDNEY HARBOR

- The Sydney Water Treatment plant is a high-tech, environmentally sound facility that processes the waste water from Sydney's businesses and residences.

- Every day, its outlet pipes release treated water into the sea. The plant is highly successful at cleaning up Sydney's wastewater, but a few hearty chunks of food, plant matter, bits of candy bar, and fish from P. Sherman's office do make it through.

- To crabs like Bernie and his pal, Baz, an outlet pipe is like a magical, never-ending, all-you-can-eat salad bar! Bernie and Baz steadfastly guard their section of the pipe, which is the best they've found in years. No wonder they only stop eating to say "Ah, sweet nectar of life."

Sydney Harbor

This is a cool place to visit if you're a human tourist, but Sydney Harbor is one mean neighborhood for a fish. If the greedy gulls don't get you, then the peckish pelicans will! When Marlin arrives at the last stage of his quest to find Nemo, he knows that reaching his son will be no picnic. If he's not careful, he'll end up as one himself!

Is that a school of moonfish practicing their impressions? No, it's the *real* Sydney Opera House!

Harbor

Sydney Harbor teems with fishing boats, ferries, cruise ships, and sailing boats. Overlooking the harbor is Sydney Harbor Bridge, known to locals as the "Coat Hanger." Dr. Sherman's boat, *The Aussie Flosser*, is moored up somewhere. Will Marlin and Dory be able to find it?

Nigel the Pelican

Nigel was hatched in a nest atop Dr. Sherman's office. At a young age, he wondered what happened to humans when they went inside. The minute he learned to fly, he perched at the window of the exam room to take a look. He has since become a dental expert, and discusses Phil Sherman's technique with the fish-tank occupants.

SYDNEY LIFE

- It isn't just the seagulls who are competitive in Sydney—the human population are very inventive at making a living, too. Check out some of their business cards....

- Wallaby Way is famous for its dentist practices and its shops selling candy—somehow the two seem to encourage each other.

- Sydney Harbor is the deepest natural harbor in the world—otherwise the whale who carried Nemo and Dory wouldn't have been able to get nearly so close.

Dr. Sherman wishes he'd got there first

UNDERWATER
SCUBA DENTISTRY
"DON'T FORGET to PANIC!"
40 Wallaby Way, Sydney, Australia

CAT & DOG **DENTISTRY**
Dr. Smiley Teeth, DDS, Vet.
44 Wallaby Way, Sydney, Australia

Not his real name

SUGAR CANDY
Specializing in Gooey-Stick-to-Your-Teeth Goodness
41 Wallab... Way, Sydney, Australia

Nigel tried to get the other pelicans interested in dentistry, but all they wanted to do was sit on top of the local bait shop and talk about how stupid seagulls were.

Tough gullet for swallowing just about anything

Webbed feet—great for catching crumbs

Hop inside my mouth if you want to live! Nigel makes Marlin an offer he can't refuse, as he takes him to find his son.

Seagulls

"Mine! Mine! Mine!" That's the cry you'll hear from the gulls down at the harbor. Each scavenger has only one goal: get what's mine and get it now! This has earned the seagulls a bad reputation with pelicans, who think they are truly rats with wings.

LONDON, NEW YORK, MUNICH,
MELBOURNE, and DELHI

ART EDITOR Guy Harvey
SENIOR EDITOR Simon Beecroft
ART DIRECTOR Mark Richards
PUBLISHING MANAGER Cynthia O'Neill Collins
CATEGORY PUBLISHER Alex Kirkham
PRODUCTION Nicola Torode
DTP DESIGNER Eric Shapland

*Peach rolls to freedom
in her plastic bag.*

Hardback Edition published in the United States, 2003
Paperback Edition published in the United States, 2004
04 05 06 07 08 10 9 8 7 6 5 4 3 2 1

Published in the United States by DK Publishing, Inc.
375 Hudson Street, New York, New York 10014

ISBN 0-7566-0483-4

A catalog record for this book is available from the Library of Congress.

Reproduced by Media Development and Printing Ltd., UK
Printed in China by Toppan Printing Co. (Shenzen) Ltd.

Acknowledgments

DK Publishing would like to thank:
Krista Swager, Leeann Alameda, Ralph Eggleston, Ricky Nierva, Ben Butcher, Bob Peterson, Shannon Brown,
Kathleen Chanover, Clay Welch, Keith Kolder, Jeff Raymond, Desiree Mourad, Blake Tucker and the Staff at
Pixar Animation Studios; Lori Heiss, Rachel Smith, Hunter Heller, Graham Barnard, and Tim Lewis at
Disney Publishing; Roger Harris for additional artworks; Steve Parker for *Eyewitness Guides: Fish* (DK Publishing)

See our complete product line at
www.dk.com